How Things Move

Fast

D1401360

Sarah Shannon

Heinemann Library
Chicago, Illinois

Editorial: Rebecca Rissman and Siân Smith
Picture research: Liz Alexander
Designed by Joanna Hinton-Malivoire
Printed and bound by South China Printing Company Limited

13 12 11 10 09
10 9 8 7 6 5 4 3 2 1

ISBN-13: 978-1-4329-2655-7 (hc)
ISBN-13: 978-1-4329-2661-8 (pb)

Library of Congress Cataloging-in-Publication Data
Shannon, Sarah.
   Fast / Sarah Shannon.
      p. cm. -- (How things move)
   Includes bibliographical references and index.
      1. Motion--Juvenile literature. 2. Force and energey--Juvenile literature. I. Title.
QC133.5.S535 2008
531'.11--dc22
                                        2008044978

Acknowledgments
The author and publisher are grateful to the following for permission to reproduce copyright material:
©Alamy pp.**12** (Alain Le Garsmeur), **11** (Andrea Bricco/ Brand X), **5** (Andy Newman/ epa), **8** (David LeBon/Transtock), **19** (David Spurdens), **7** (G. Bowater), **13** (Juice Images), **9** (Kevin Dodge), **4** (Lester Lefkowitz), **10** (Steve Prezant), **20** (Tom Brakefield), **14** (Wally McNamee); ©Getty Images. p.**17 right** (Gallo Images/Martin Harvey); ©iStockphoto.com pp.**6** (Kseniya Abramova), **17 left** (Heather Down); ©Photolibrary pp.**18** (Wolfgang Weinhäupl/Mauritius), **21** (Mauritius), **16** (Nonstock/ Fabrik-Studios Ltd), **15** (Stockbyte/Photodisc).

Cover photograph of a yellow car reproduced with permission of ©Corbis (David Madison). Back cover photograph of a waterskier reproduced with permission of ©Photolibrary (Stockbyte/Photodisc).

Every effort has been made to contact copyright holders of any material reproduced in this book. Any omissions will be rectified in subsequent printings if notice is given to the publisher.

Contents

Moving

Things move in many ways.

Things move in many places.

Moving Fast

Some things can move fast.

A train can move fast.

A car can move fast.

A person can move fast.

Pushes

A push can make things move fast.

When you push a swing it moves fast.

Pulls

A pull can make things move fast.

When you pull a sled it moves fast.

Moving Faster

A big push can make something move faster.

A big pull can make something move faster.

A car is faster than a bicycle.

A cheetah is faster than a slug.

As a sled speeds up, it gets faster and faster.

As a plane speeds up, it gets faster and faster.

Fast Things

Things can move fast.

You can move fast.

What Have You Learned?

- Things can move fast.

- Pushes and pulls can make things move fast.

- A big push can make something move faster.

- A big pull can make something move faster.

Picture Glossary

 **pull** to make something move towards you

 **push** to make something move away from you

Index

Note to Parents and Teachers

Before reading

Talk to children about different ways to move. Sometimes we move fast and sometimes we move slowly. Ask the children for examples of when they move fast (playing football, running races, riding a bike) or slowly (in a crowded shop, waiting in line). What things can they think of that move very fast? Make a list on the board.

After reading

• Let children roll toy cars down a ramp. Which car goes the farthest? Which car goes the quickest? Make the ramp steeper. Will the cars go faster or slower? Why?

• Tell children to look through magazines and catalogs. They should cut out pictures of things that move fast. Then they should agree which things go the fastest. Paste these on a poster in order of speed.